The Zeitgeist:
A Journey of Reflections

Dr. Deepikaa Rupert Gardner

BookLeaf
Publishing

India | USA | UK

Presentation by *BookLeaf Publishing*

Web: www.bookleafpub.com

E-mail: info@bookleafpub.com

ISBN: 9789363319158

First edition 2024

Dedicated to my Parents -

Rajnikant Neelkanth Rao Nagarkar and
Veena Rajnikanth Nagarkar

ACKNOWLEDGEMENT

I would like to express my gratitude to the publishers of Book Leaf Publishing who inspired me to take up this venture. #TheWriteAngle Writing Challenge.

PREFACE

Poetry to me is the expression of the deeply felt emotions of my soul.

The visual beauty that surrounds us everywhere and the memories of people pour out through the pen describing and overflowing with words that touch my soul. The words that gush forth are the consequences of my varied experiences of life. The lens through which I view the world is what I have tried to express here. It has quite a few poems reflecting on this aspect. I kind of feel it's the blueprint of my life.

Zeitgeist means the general intellectual, moral, and cultural climate of an era. *It comes from the German word- "Zeit" means 'time' and geist means 'spirit'- The Spirit of the Times.*

Human emotions are shaped by the socio-cultural conditions which one faces during the entire journey of life. These words are molded by our senses, desires, wishes, and reminiscences. We remember, recall, and recollect the memorable times and words start flowing on the paper. The memories can be of good times or painful events that happen all around us leaving an indelible mark on the mind.

My book is written in free verse (as I feel it is) -which is a form of poetry that does not follow the traditional patterns of rhyme, meter, or structure. It allows poets to create fluid pieces without any rules or constraints. You will find varied line lengths and words that convey meaning and emotion as per my mood. They are more like spoken words or conversations. Free verse permits greater creativity and flexibility to experiment with unique ways of language and expression with a very personal touch.

This is an extremely popular choice and format today for a spontaneous authentic voice for people like me. In the depths of my soul, where words dance with emotions and thoughts echo with love and pain, there lies the realm of my poetic experience. My life has been quite tragic and yet with support, hard work, and God's guidance, I could accomplish great targets. It is within these verses that I find solace, understanding, and sometimes even the mirror reflecting my innermost self.

The Zeitgeist is more than just a collection of poems; it is a journey into the heart of existence of our times. Each line is a delicate thread, woven to capture the flow of emotions as I pass through the repertoire of my experiences. These poems strive to articulate what often eludes mere language: the whispers of our souls, the vast spectrum of trends, the challenging societal norms, the multidimensional new normal, and finding identity and meaning in a fragmented world.

You will encounter a spectrum of human emotions to explore, to feel, and to connect. They beckon you to dive into the depths of your own being, to confront the truths that reside within, and to emerge with a renewed sense of understanding and acceptance.
As you embark on this poetic journey, may you find resonance in these whispers of my soul!

May they speak to you in moments of solitude and accompany you in moments of reflection. May they remind you that, amidst the chaos of life, there is always beauty to be found in the cadence of words and the melody of the human spirit.

The Zeitgeist

Living in a modern city or town
Life today can almost drown
This is the digital age
That can virtually go upstage

We're chasing shadows on our screens
We're connected virtually in memes
Reality has a huge disconnect
In-person conversations are in total neglect

Intolerance is rampant today
Patience isn't here to stay
Parents are killing children without mercy
Insensitivity has become a controversy

For trivial things, people are killing
Anger and stress are so damn spine chilling
Situations lead to this mental imbalance

Crimes shooting up and indicating distrust and
malice
People are seeking justice constantly
Also trying to justify instantly
What do they do and why
How they do and why

Selfie-mania is killing Gen Zers
From the top of the cliffs
Or on the roads
Taking selfies or making reels

Road rage is ubiquitous today
Social media is full of these today
An overload of vehicular traffic
With the dearth of time and impatience most
graphic

Plants and trees have suffered for long
Silently screaming and crying decades-long
Now Nature's furious and punitive
With heat and flash floods iterative

Cars are burning, and so are the buildings
Men are dying, others are filming
The blatant warnings and signals of doom
Greed and selfishness have a blind boom

Unemployment and crimes increasing
Morals and values decreasing
If this is what our children see
Tomorrow, we'll all be at sea

People are immune to human suffering
Not immune to virus or bacterial suffering
Scripting history hitherto unknown
Moving into zones yet unknown

Loneliness assumes a gigantic proportion
Relationships are deceitful distortion
Often founded on fraud and lies
Zeitgeist is fool's paradise!

Behind every smiling face
Isn't a happy ace
Why did he commit suicide?
His Insta profile showed a rich, happy side

Well, if you must know
He was utterly lonely bro
With five billion followers
But no real close cronies

The zeitgeist sings a warning song
Wars creating mourning so long

Restless beings killing man and Nature alike
Why is humanity a beastly spike?

Heed the Zeitgeist's present plea
For destiny to foresee
Be mindful of life's intricacy
Leave the world a good legacy

NATURE

Beauty Abounds

The azure blue of the sky
Bright flowers and green trees vie
The cool, crisp air
Whisper the Nilgiris care

The beauty astounds
Natural wealth abounds
The greeneries attract
The numerous fields intact

There's beauty wherever your eyes turn
There's magic and love in every churn
That fills your heart with joy
To be alive and here today!

Climate Crisis

Just as people throw a tantrum
When things become a humdrum
I guess, nature too has an angry form
What else is the frequent dust storm?

It's Nature's way of showing its disgust
For the wrongs of men with dust and cloud
bursts
What's climate change then?
It's Nature's fury in response to the callous men

Flash floods destroy everything en route
The watery graves of humans mute
Indiscriminate destruction of property
Nature's way to deal with impropriety

It's a WAKE-UP CALL for us
A Clarion Call for sustainability plus
To bring PEACE to Nature and creatures on
earth
Before it's too late for what it is worth!!!

The Nurturer: Sun

The sun has great potential
It is a giver
Giving the essential light
Giving the warmth to a shiver

Day after day it gives
Never tardy in its duty
Year after year it gives
Never shirking its responsibility

It teaches a great lesson
If you care to learn
To be like the sun in heaven
To be like the sun- ready to burn

The warmth in winter
On chilly rainy days
Provides fire and timber
To creatures on earth all days

Nature

The greatest teacher of the world is Nature
The flowers give out a fragrance
Fruit-laden trees humble nature
The mountains have a firm semblance

Trees give shade and fruit selflessly
The clouds rain abundantly
The sun is the big day lamp
The moon the small night lamp

Nature's cycle teaches consistency
Timely flowering discipline
Revolving planets teach work-consistency
Always on the wheel spin

Nature is God's way of teaching a life lesson
Care to emulate?
Be humble, consistent, and sincere to earn
God's blessings sooner than later

The Stormy Night

The night seemed to stretch
The clock ticking with an edge
I was engrossed in my book
Waiting patiently for the cook

I slowly put my book down
Went to the window quietly
And looked with a frown
The clouds moving quickly

It seemed to be a dark dull night
I longed for the countless small stars
The lamps decorated the sky with light
Alas! They were nowhere that night

Then all of a sudden the strong wind
Blew rattling the door and window
The leaves rustled and whined
It was a thunderstorm below

I went back to my bed
Wishing for rain tread
Despite the noisy storm howling
I fell into a restless sleep scowling

Dawn came after a few hours
Displaying the fury of the showers
Gentle raindrops quietly fell
On the uprooted trees and well

The electric poles had fallen
Buildings showed signs of devastation too
Many vehicles were damaged
By the uprooted fallen trees mangled

Man, wake up! If not now, then when?
Treat Nature respectfully
For the next-gen
To live happily and peacefully

The Sweltering Day

Human beings have desecrated
Nature for so many decades
Now the boundaries have been crossed
Nature is cross with man's escapades

The fury of Nature is mighty visible
In multiple ways
The raging forest fires seem invincible
The flash floods furiously cause frays

The strong sun is shining relentlessly
As if pouring out its anger undoubtedly On all
mankind indiscriminately
The fury in its heat killing men mercilessly

Celebrate birthdays by planting a tree

So many birthdays are celebrated every day
Imagine how green the earth will be
Gen-next will live peacefully if we do this
today!

The clarion call of today is to
Be aware of these moods of Nature
Plant trees, save water, and save us
Before it is too big a failure!!!

Mother Nature

Saving our planet is not an option
Protecting the environment is not a choice
Taking care of this creation
Is an urgent voice

Our lives depend on sustainable choice
We live and breathe because of Nature
Survival, therefore, is the best noise
Sustainability is our true nature

Plants, animals, and human beings
All thrive because of a balance
We need balance for our children's bearings
We need it to rectify the imbalance

Learn and teach a lesson in sustainable choices
Being superior in the natural kingdom Man has
irresponsibly destroyed the delicate choices The
onus lies upon us to rectify this kingdom

Let's take a pledge to plant a tree every day
Let's promise to nurture them every day Let's
teach small children through our work
To love, respect, and nurture the plant turf

LIFE

Life's an Enigma

Life's an enigma
Forever deluding us
There are lights and shadows
There are mysterious meadows

The dawn and dusk
The ups and downs
Whisper secrets in silence
Eluding human guidance

The more we try to unravel life
The more the tapestry of life
It gets intricate and intriguing
Mesmerizing and alluring

A Rainbow of Emotions

We are emotional creatures
Feeling a rainbow of emotional features
Sometimes we cannot decipher them
Sometimes we're overwhelmed by them

Life gives us a rainbow of emotions
To decode the myriad notions
Sometimes it is a Herculean task
Sometimes just a simple ask

Children must identify emotions
Must understand the expressions
Should know reasons for feeling them
Learn to manage them effectively

This teaches them to be in control
To learn to navigate through the rigmarole
The turbulent sea of emotions
To land them safely in their roles

Each emotion must be labelled
Each emotion scrutinized
Each trigger for emotion unravelled
All emotions to be analysed

Emotional balance gives strength
To gauge life's length
Emotions are vital
Must be handled well for survival!

Let's Live Today

Let's not worry about
The tomorrows
Let's live our lives in bouts
In the present without doubt

What you do today
Will affect your tomorrow
So live well today
For a better tomorrow

It's our deeds today
That shapes our tomorrow
So sow good seeds today
To reap good fruits tomorrow

Our preps and actions today
Directly affect our future someday
So do good deeds today
To have your dreams fulfilled someday

The Urbanites

We don't know our neighbours
We live in high-rise apartments
Our doors are always shut
Our hearts are also shut

We are urbanites, we see
An accident on the road but cannot see
We hurriedly walk by
 It's no one I know, I must walk by

Why should I stop and help
It's a stranger I can't help
Some are making videos
Why should I bother? It's a weirdo

Urban life has made our hearts rock-hard
We're insensitive and scarred to
Human suffering and vulnerabilities
We are urbanites...we live in cities...

Unleash!

Mind is the powerhouse
Of energy and intellect
Mind it is that's the remote to
Unleash its power!

Unleash the power and
Discover the glorious designs
Discover the beauty and colours
Discover the fragrance of life!

Suppress not, worry not
Mind is resilient
It is the powerhouse
That lights up your life!!!

Music

Music brings peace and heals the soul
Transports you into another realm
Melody surpasses the boundaries of the soul
Makes you dance with glee under the elm

Music knows no language
It does not cause damage
Music lovers revel in the melody
Just as everyone enjoys Nature's rhapsody

It heals, mends, and repairs the broken
Hearts and souls it has woken
It's wonderful in its rendering
All music lovers are surrendering

Mental Well-being

Stress is driving us to the wall
Anxiety is increasing day by day
There's no quick fix for this fall
It's driving people crazy today

This will soon turn into a pandemic
Of gigantic proportion
Unless we pause and reflect on this epidemic
Humanity is at stake with this distortion

Tomorrow, my friend would be too late
Do what you can today
As long as the waves can't manipulate
Else nobody can stop the Tsunami any day

If You Love Your Nation…

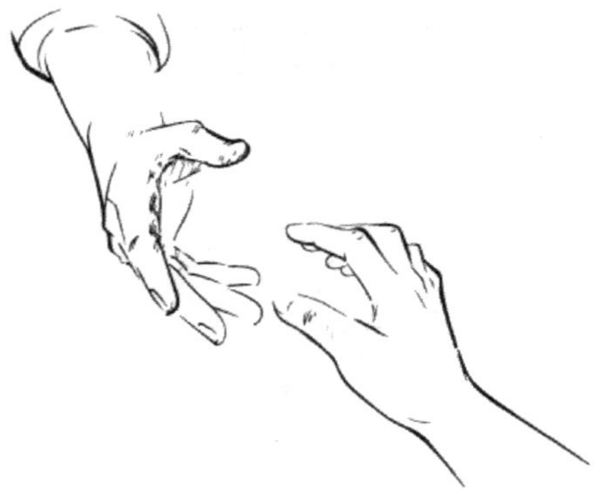

If you love your nation
Then take care of the notion
Love, friendship, and brotherhood
Take care of each other from childhood

Be child-like
Shun hatred
Arrogance, envy, and anger alike
Deconstruct hatred

Peace, love, and goodwill
Must always persist
War, enmity, and ill-will
Must always desist

Do not destroy the nation
In the name of religion
For every religion teaches you
To respect others like you

For every religion teaches you
To love your nation
For every religion teaches you
To also love and respect the other nation

Transformative Servant Leadership

This is the kind of leadership
That is the hour's kinship
Leaders aren't kings
People are the kings

Leaders are made to serve not be served
Right transformative signals are served
Through service, all learn
To be better leaders who earn

Good role modeling is required
For the future of the world
Education and wisdom are required
Not just fake degrees hurled

People with degrees might be fake
What use is knowledge if it's a mistake?
The world doesn't need educated illiterates
It needs people who are wise and considerate

It needs people who can think intelligently
Who can make decisions quickly
Who can transform the world collectively
By leading people to progress wisely

It needs people who can think rationally
It needs people who can work selflessly
It needs people who aren't arrogant
It needs people who aren't simply negligent

It needs leaders who can empathize
It needs leaders who can sympathize
It needs leaders with compassion and solutions
It needs leaders to bring revolutions!

Lifestyle

How do we live today?
I wish it were the good old days today
When we walked and worked with our hands
When machines were not our brands'

Life was healthier and easier then
When we did our work then
Today we have readymade help
Visits to the hospital need self-help

The human body is a machine too
It needs exercise in its purview
To keep it running smoothly, lest it stops
Do that exercise and don't just hop

Lifestyle changes are needed urgently
To correct and work diligently
Lest it is too late to mend

Lest we fall into the diseased blend

Lest we need the vicious rounds to the hospital
Lest we do irreparable harm and become critical
Lest we lose our mental balance and dignity
Lest we miss out on our lives till eternity

Gen Z: The Powerhouse of Talent

The problem with our generation is
 that they don't understand Gen Z
Posing challenges for this generation
Traditional work environs aren't for Gen Z

The plight of Gen Z
Are the parents, professors, and employers
None of them understand Gen Z
Ultimately, there are no takers

I being a mother and teacher
Could build a rapport with them
I engaged them as a friendly teacher
To help gel with them

I could always tackle any kind of student
Could relate to their problem
Counsel and hone their talent
Proud to see my students blossom

They bring a fresh perspective
With digital prowess
Navigating and introspective
Handling technology with ease and prowess

They drive innovation with unique insights
They're a powerhouse of talents
Unexplored and raw talents
Transcending all boundaries with pageants

Give them a seat at the table
Give them a chance to voice their idea
Let them create a dynamic label
Where new talent begets growth and media

Lend them an empathetic ear
Support them when they need it
Remove from them the fear
Give them a part and act it

They are the innovators of tomorrow
They are the leaders of tomorrow
Let their talent shine forth
Let them lead us to a glorious tomorrow

Embrace Stress

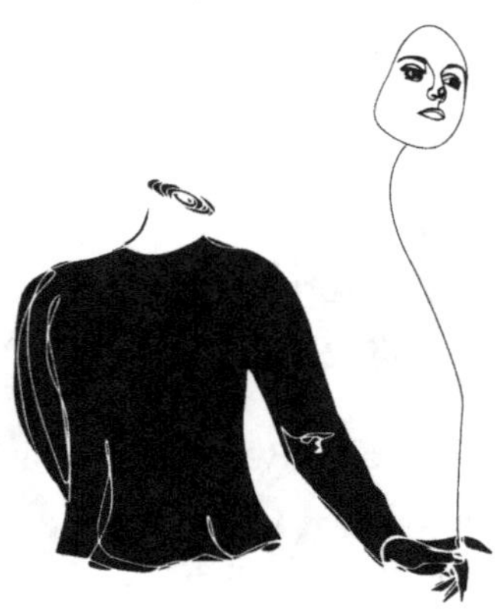

Seriously heed my advice
Embrace stress too
Don't we embrace things when people criticize?
Well, stress happens to be part of our lives too

Stress is important for us
To keep procrastination at bay
It stops complacency from us
To be vigilant and make our way

Stress leads us to anxiety
Anxiety is necessary as it
helps us to move forward and
Complete what we started

Life would be dull
If we aren't worrying and warring
Worry, and reflection on our situation
Lead us to success, driving away anxiety

Climate Cruelty to Women

As with everything else with women
Climate plays havoc with women
Whether it's scorching summer or chilly winter
Icy lashing rains or inclement weather

Women don't just have to worry 'bout them
But also family at the helm
need to be protected and taken care of
Family needs to be taken care of

Women though popularly called the weaker sex
Are much stronger sex
Both mentally and physically

As they bear the entire burden cheerfully

No Sundays or other days are holidays
They must sleep late and get up early all days
To make things rolling smoothly
Salute and respect them profusely!

AUTOBIOGRAPHICAL SECTION

Early Joyful Childhood

Early childhood is a crucial time
In a child's and parents' lifetime
The child's adulthood depends on it
 The child's rest of the life depends on it

From birth to eight years the time is critical
A child's physical and social
Cognitive and emotional
Growth happens at this time typical

The trajectory of a child's life depends
Upon how he was taken care of
What and how he was taught extends
To how his experiences were taken care of

If a child is appreciated in their childhood
He learns to praise others
If he's encouraged in childhood
He inspires and encourages others

If he learns to lose gracefully
He learns to accept things with equanimity
If he's taught hard work purposefully
He values it with sublimity

Parents- teach and model good things
To help your child grow well
To make your child emotionally strong
To make him mentally resilient and dwell

Teach your child to think
Give him a chance to express
Give him a chance to make decisions in a blink
Teach him to face life's storms without stress

Charming Childhood

As a child, you want to grow big soon
Yet when you do grow big soon
You long for your happy childhood
Instead of just working for livelihood

Those were beautiful days
Full of precious memories
They continually haunt us
In the prime of our lives

The best part was the train journey to Nani's
house
The huge sprawling railway bungalow in
Gangapur City
A treat we longed for in summers to browse
Life was at another tangent in that small city

My Nana- a mail guard was handsome in his
crisp white
Railway uniform and shining brass lamp
Was a strict disciplinarian yet he loved us right
He has been a pillar of support and a guiding
lamp

Nani, on the other hand, was sweetness
personified
A beautiful Cambridge educated dignified lady
Loved us no end and watching her at work was a
pleasure personified
She cooked the world's most delicious food
ever!

She would smile and tell stories of her young
days
She had learned horse riding as a young girl
In Lucknow during the British rule days
Surely her father had pampered the young girl

Come summer that railway bungalow came alive
With daughter's and grandchildren's laughter
Chatting, running, humming like a beehive
Those were the cherished days full of laughter

The big hen house was a fascination
From where we collected eggs
And held the little yellow chicks in jubilation

Awestruck by their beauty and softness

The guava trees on which we climbed up and
down
The huge playground to run freely
In the afternoons the cabins to play around
Loaded with fun and funny tales recounted airily

The Sparkling Eyes

When I look into those eyes
Those beautiful shiny eyes
I feel mesmerized by those eyes
Those sparkling eyes

His smile, so captivating
His face, so sweet and inviting
He'll hold you captive by
Those sparkling eyes

He's only four months old
Yet conveys the joy of gold
Through his expressive eyes
Those sparkling eyes

Eyes that communicate
His naughtiness and glee
Oh! He is so cute and adorable
With those sparkling eyes

Happiness writ all over
His charming face with a cute cleft in his chin
His eyes tell tales of happiness and glee
Those sparkling eyes

Your heart melts with his smile
Your defenses are down
You are held captive by the beauty of
Those sparkling eyes

Grateful to the maker
For this big blessing in our lives
He is so delightful and loving
With those sparkling eyes!!!

The Good Shepherd

Amidst the beauty of the Nilgiris
On the sprawling acres of land
Stands the majestic Good Shepherd
Surveying the vicinity all around

The serene little Chapel
With the bright flowers all around
Is a balm for the aching soul
Who can be sad amidst all this wealth of Nature?

The tall concrete buildings
Are not just cement, bricks, and sand
They are the hopes, aspirations and
Joys of many generations to come

These buildings are not just walls and roofs
They are alive with love and proof

of a dedicated founder
And the members of the Good Shepherd

O Dear Good Shepherd
'Tis but a small prayer
Let the school attain its full glory
Under your gentle care

With your love and blessings
Under your kind biddance
And right guidance
Let it always flourish!

The Transient Life

As I stroll down the memory lane
Lives and events flash by in a chain
Moments of glee and grief
Hours of love and care brief

Moments whisper as they flit by
Don't let life fly by
Live and love fully today
For tomorrow may not come by

Life is transient
Men are complacent
Bearing grudges against each other
Hard and unforgiving brother

Yet, in a moment life is snuffed out
The departed souls reach out
To convey forgive, forget, and move on
To forgive, forget, and move on...

Carry no baggage, for empty-handed we depart
Live well, while there is time to restart
Laugh and be carefree
Care and be carefree

Learn to live happily today
Be grateful for your family on this day
For today is everything
For tomorrow may never come...

My Beautiful Mother

Mother, I have not yet reconciled myself
With your sudden passing away
You were the pillar of my strength, my smiles,
and my self
It's been a decade since...

You have I loved and respected
For your courage and resilience
Ever since I can remember you displayed
Tolerance and forbearance
It's been a decade since...

You mother, were my support system
You knew my needs even before I uttered
You made a brave and strong system
It's been a decade since...

With my parents, siblings, relatives, and good
neighbours
Late-night music soirees of my favourite ghazals

And then there was this 'lil zoo with a tortoise
and few fish in the pond
A faithful dog and two rabbits with a frond
A parrot and two 'lil Siamese kittens bullied by
the parrot...
The fragrant garden full of roses, jasmine,
zinnias, and carrot

Bungalow No. 12 was a sight to behold
Etched in my memory deep...on hold
I miss you for your beauty and serenity
I'll hold my precious memories till eternity
Of childhood, adulthood, and my parents!!!

Dad, I Miss you!

My dad- was a formidable man
As small kids, we feared the man
He looked handsome in his Khaki uniform
His powerful voice could transform

Every time he called out
I used to run out
Though admired him from a distance
With his pistol in its holster

He taught me Sanskrit
And I learned with grit
He made me memorize
The shlokas for my exam I realize

He taught me to ride my bicycle
He would run behind my cycle
Pretending to hold my bike
But I was balancing my bike

He always told my mother not to refuse
Anything I wanted to buy
He wanted girls to be happy in their refuge
No one knew what the future could supply

I wish parents today understand this
For many girls are suffering and dying today
Let them at least be happy in their own homes
today
Give your daughters beautiful and memorable
bliss!

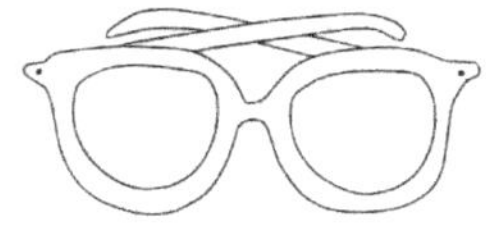

My Alma Mater

As I stand on the threshold
A thousand memories come crowding
The beautiful and blissful memories on hold
Of yester years come crowding

Memories of seniors, batch mates, and
professors
The fun in the hostel with seniors
The lectures, the labs, the cooking samsara
The 5 am yoga and Surya Namaskara

The Youth Fest First Prize for Western Vocal
The CTAE and RCA Hindi movies
Shopping sprees in Bapu Bazar and shops local
The restaurant's food and theatre movies

Thanking everyone for their contribution
In making these memories sweeter
And Golden Jubilee Celebrations 2016
completer
Made it gratifying and richer with fun!

You were My Universe

In the heart of darkness
I look for the flame
In the sound of the wind
I listen for your name
I stop and realize...You are all things to me...

I wait for your footsteps
Listen to the traffic sounds
Wait for the buzz to quieten
To hear you come and awaken
I stop and realize...You are all things to me...

I waited in vain
You never came back again
I was distraught with misery and grief
My heart filled with sorrow and disbelief
I stopped and realized...You were all things to
me...

I cried and cried
I blocked my mind
I took to books
Worked in nooks
I stopped and realized…
You were all things to me...

I worked unceasingly
and Took care of the children carefully
Mother was a stronghold
My anchor and my household
I stop and realize...You were all things to me...

Being a Language Teacher

I had never wanted to be a teacher
and Turned down training to be a teacher
I wanted to pursue law inspired by my dad
Circumstances proved challenging and mad

I was an avid reader so logically I did my
Masters in English faithfully Fulfilled my
mother's dream
Started teaching in college team

I hadn't realized that teaching
Was a legacy from the family days
It was right there in the genes waiting
Began peer teaching, in my undergrad days

Teaching I realized, was not about finances
It was all about your commitment
To the student fraternity
It was how you influenced infinity

Teaching is building mental bridges
Empowering young lives
It is academic parenting
Giving a part of yourself mentoring

I'm grateful for having great teachers
My parents, grandparents, aunts, and uncles
Then my KVN teachers I salute along with
My professors at all levels

Rest is my voracious appetite for reading
And zeal for learning
Books were always the rock-solid foundation
Learning from my students the next elation
University of Cambridge the Ultimate!!!

My Treasure

My children are my treasure
Nothing can ever measure
How much is the pleasure
To see this great treasure

Life really has been uphill
But these two made it thrill
It's such a big blessing
To count my manifold blessings

Many thanks to the Creator
Always guide and safeguard them
There is no prayer greater
Everywhere and always be with them!

World Champs!

India's scripted history again
And deservedly so…
These moments of sheer brilliance
Make our 'Men in Blue' unique

There have been all kinds of moments
But this has been Momentous!
Good or bad, happy or sad
These are unforgettable

Hard work, resilience and brilliance
All rolled into one
The Men in Blue!
Their perseverance is the glue

Together they could do it
Together they'll do it again
A feat to remember
A victory to savour!!!

Basic Fundas

Learn to communicate expertly
In written, oral and visual communication
Be a skilled negotiator
Above all an active listener

These will tide you over
In rough layoff season
For transferable skills
Relate to every job, every reason

Lose neither your sanity nor confidence
These are just life's rough patches
Be of good cheer
For your skills shall be your catches

Mind your hourglass for it's important
Upgrade your skillset 'tis important
Keep learning and relearning
To be able to keep earning

Life's Essence

Life's essence lies in hard work
It lies in perseverance
We have the ability
To bounce back from failures

Know the power of resilience
Learn to work with perseverance
If sometimes it doesn't work
Start all over with due diligence

Be glad, for the blessings
Be glad, for the opportunities
Be glad, for this life and work
Be glad, for what it's worth

Empathy

Can you hear me?
Can you really hear me?
I need some sympathy
With a dash of empathy

Come, sit and talk to me now
With my manager, I had a row
Isn't there a time for layoffs?
How can there be a season of layoffs?

What will I tell my baby?
How will I manage the expenses?
The salary cheque's gone
What to tell parents and spouse on the phone?

Micro Poems

75

Dreamz

Dreamz are the stuff
That my life is made of
Wake up n they go snuff
They're just dreamz…

Digitally Yourz

It's a digital full toss
Taking its toll
Mind is slippery as moss
Can I ever stand tall?

My Cell Phone

I haven't been sleeping
The phone keeps ringing
Life's pages are flipping
I cannot be dreaming

Moments

Life's made up of moments
Moments are slipping by
Try to seek help nearby
Running in almost circles

Muddle

Confusion, anger and despair
Against society so unfair
Look around for help
Cry, whine and whelp!

Bewilderment

My mind is all puzzled
My lens is getting blurred
My voice is getting slurred
I can no longer hope for help!

Wait

Can you wait for me?
If only for a moment
If you cannot see
I'll understand it

Differently-abled

I am differently-abled
I need no pity or sympathy
I need support so I can work and be able
I need help and some empathy